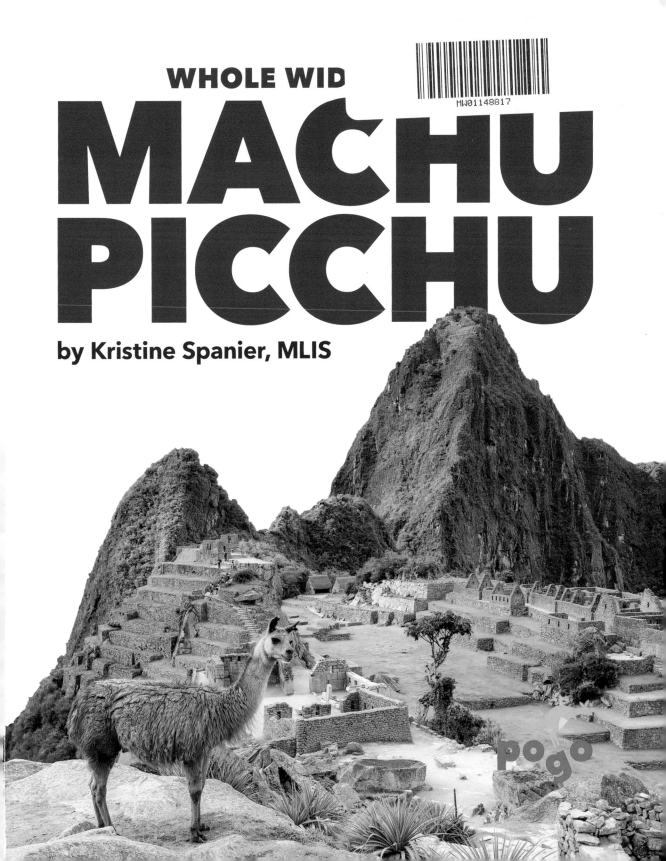

WHOLE WID
MACHU PICCHU

by Kristine Spanier, MLIS

pogo

Ideas for Parents and Teachers

Pogo Books let children practice reading informational text while introducing them to nonfiction features such as headings, labels, sidebars, maps, and diagrams, as well as a table of contents, glossary, and index.

Carefully leveled text with a strong photo match offers early fluent readers the support they need to succeed.

Before Reading

• "Walk" through the book and point out the various nonfiction features. Ask the student what purpose each feature serves.

• Look at the glossary together. Read and discuss the words.

Read the Book

• Have the child read the book independently.

• Invite him or her to list questions that arise from reading.

After Reading

• Discuss the child's questions. Talk about how he or she might find answers to those questions.

• Prompt the child to think more. Ask: What did you know about Machu Picchu before you read this book? What more would you like to learn?

Pogo Books are published by Jump!
5357 Penn Avenue South
Minneapolis, MN 55419
www.jumplibrary.com

Library of Congress Cataloging-in-Publication Data

Names: Spanier, Kristine, author.
Title: Machu Picchu / by Kristine Spanier.
Description: Minneapolis: Jump!, Inc., 2021.
Series: Whole wide world | Includes index.
Audience: Ages 7-10 | Audience: Grades 2-3
Identifiers: LCCN 2020027759 (print)
LCCN 2020027760 (ebook)
ISBN 9781645277415 (hardcover)
ISBN 9781645277422 (paperback)
ISBN 9781645277439 (ebook)
Subjects: LCSH: Machu Picchu Site (Peru —Juvenile literature. | Peru—Antiquities—Juvenile literature.
Incas—History—Juvenile literature.
Inca architecture—Juvenile literature.
Classification: LCC F3429.1.M3 S67 2021 (print)
LCC F3429.1.M3 (ebook) | DDC 985/.01—dc23
LC record available at https://lccn.loc.gov/2020027759
LC ebook record available at https://lccn.loc.gov/2020027760

Editor: Jenna Gleisner
Designer: Molly Ballanger

Photo Credits: Seumas Christie-Johnston/Shutterstock, cover; Don Mammoser/Shutterstock, 1; Angela Villavicencio Varg/Shutterstock, 3; John Warburton Lee/SuperStock, 4; SL_Photography/iStock, 5; emperorcosar/Shutterstock, 6-7; SI Photography/Shutterstock, 8; Armando Frazao/Shutterstock, 9; lu_sea/Shutterstock, 10-11; 3fairyz/Shutterstock, 11 (map); Marek Poplawski/Dreamstime, 12-13; Paolo Costa/Shutterstock, 14-15; legacy1995/iStock, 16-17; cge2010/Shutterstock, 18; Lordprice Collection/Alamy, 19; meunierd/Shutterstock, 20-21; Kirill Trifonov/Dreamstime, 23.

Printed in the United States of America at Corporate Graphics in North Mankato, Minnesota.

TABLE OF CONTENTS

CHAPTER 1

STONE VILLAGE

Take a trip 50 miles (80 kilometers) northwest of Cusco, Peru. Hike up the Inca Trail. Walk through the Sun Gate. You are at Machu Picchu!

Sun Gate

Huayna Picchu

This site is at an **elevation** of 7,972 feet (2,430 meters). It is in the Andes Mountains. It is between two mountains. One is Huayna Picchu. The other is Machu Picchu.

Machu Picchu

The site covers about 80,000 acres (32,375 hectares). Around 200 stone **structures** are here. The Inca people built them more than 500 years ago.

This site may have been a **retreat** for Inca **royalty**. They traveled here. Priests led ceremonies. Common people lived here, too.

DID YOU KNOW?

The Incas lived in an area that includes what is now Peru. They controlled an **empire** starting in the 1400s.

CHAPTER 2

A PLACE FOR EVERYONE

The holy **district** showcased the sun. Why? It was **sacred** to the Incas. The Hitching Post of the Sun is here. It is a **sundial**. It tracked the path of the sun. This told people when to hold special events.

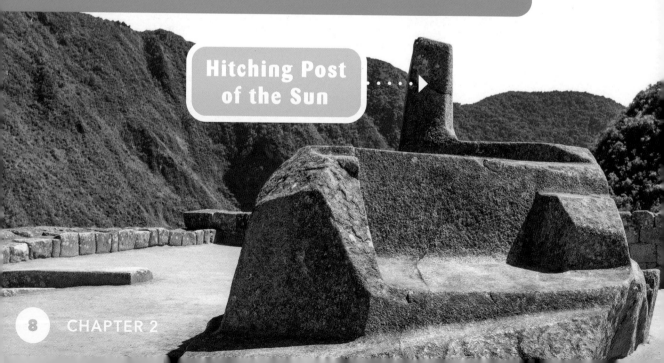

Hitching Post of the Sun

Temple of
the Sun

The Temple of the Sun
is the only round building
here. The sun shines on a
stone in the center during
the winter **solstice**.

This is the Temple of the Three Windows. What did people see when they looked through them? Each one framed a mountain.

window

TAKE A LOOK!

Around 200 structures are here. Where are some of them? Take a look!

❶ **Hitching Post of the Sun**
❷ **Temple of the Three Windows**
❸ **Temple of the Sun**

Common people lived in the popular district. Small houses were built in groups. A plaza is near each group. This was a gathering place. Grain and corn were stored nearby.

popular district

trapezoid

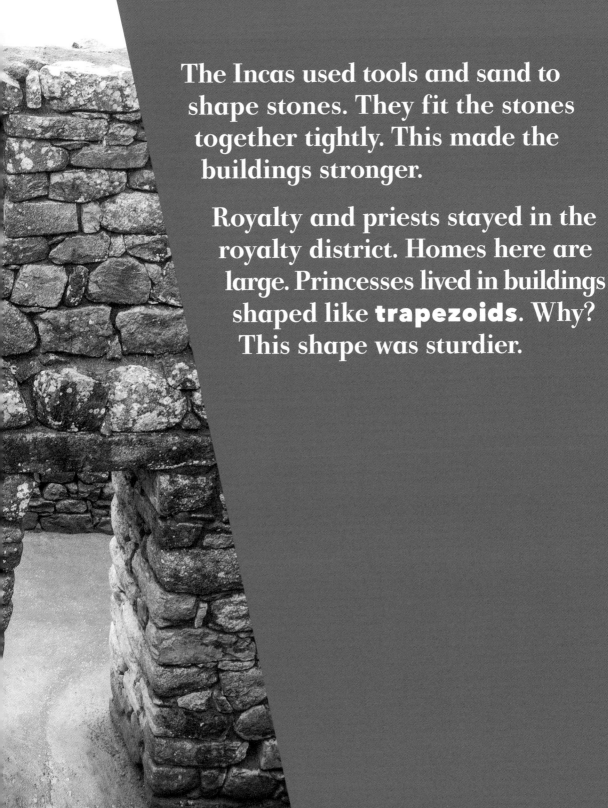

The Incas used tools and sand to shape stones. They fit the stones together tightly. This made the buildings stronger.

Royalty and priests stayed in the royalty district. Homes here are large. Princesses lived in buildings shaped like **trapezoids**. Why? This shape was sturdier.

Farmers grew **crops** on **terraces**. Terraces allowed for more growing space. The farmers lived nearby.

They also engineered fountains. There are 16. Rainwater flowed into them. People filled clay jugs with the water.

WHAT DO YOU THINK?

The Inca people drank the water they collected. What else do you think they used the water for?

terrace · · · · ▶

CHAPTER 3

THE RUINS TODAY

The Spanish arrived around 1532. What they found was a city left behind. Jungle had grown around it.

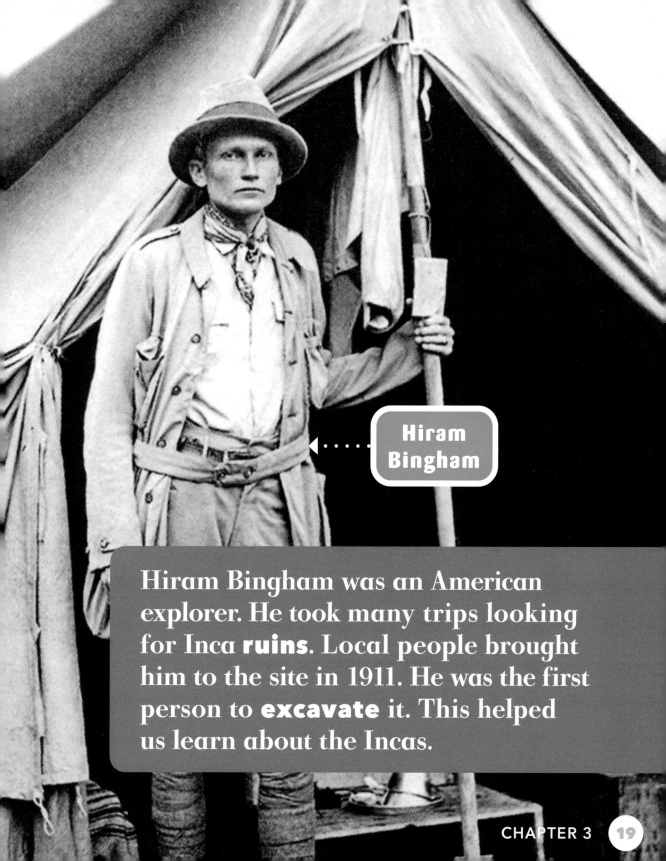

Hiram Bingham

Hiram Bingham was an American explorer. He took many trips looking for Inca **ruins**. Local people brought him to the site in 1911. He was the first person to **excavate** it. This helped us learn about the Incas.

Machu Picchu is an important place for the people of Peru. Visitors can take a train from Cusco. A bus takes them up the mountain. Some people hike up the Inca Trail. This can take four days! Do you want to visit the ruins?

WHAT DO YOU THINK?

Many people want to visit. But the government wants to keep the area protected. It limits visitors. Do you think this is a good idea? Why or why not?

QUICK FACTS & TOOLS

MACHU PICCHU

Location: Andes Mountains, Peru

Size: 80,000 acres (32,375 hectares)

Years Built (estimate): 1400 to 1450

Past Use: royal retreat

Current Use: cultural site and visitor attraction

Number of Visitors Each Year: around 1.5 million

GLOSSARY

crops: Plants grown for food.

district: An area or region.

elevation: The height above sea level.

empire: A group of countries or states that have the same ruler.

excavate: To dig in the earth to search for something that is buried.

retreat: A place where you can go to relax or be alone.

royalty: A king or queen or members of his or her family.

ruins: The remains of something that has collapsed or been destroyed.

sacred: Holy or having to do with religion.

solstice: The moment of time during the year when the overhead sun reaches its farthest point north or south of the equator.

structures: Things that have been built.

sundial: An instrument that shows the time with a pointer that casts a shadow on a flat dial similar to the face of a clock.

terraces: Leveled areas that resemble a series of steps.

trapezoids: Shapes with four sides of which only two are parallel.

INDEX

TO LEARN MORE

Finding more information is as easy as 1, 2, 3.

❶ Go to www.factsurfer.com

❷ Enter "MachuPicchu" into the search box.

❸ Choose your book to see a list of websites.

FACT SURFER